Forty Days

Of

Grace

by
Wendell VanValin

dedicated to
H. Wayne Hunter

Forty Days of Grace is published by Shoot from the Hip Publication, Bowling Green, KY

Printed in the United States of America

Contact Wendell at wvanvalin@broadwayunited.org

All scriptures paraphrased by author and appear in italics.

Written by - Wendell VanValin

Editing - Robbie VanValin

Cover and layout design by Cheryl Iaquinta
Cover background image by JuergenPM
Cover horse image by Erdenebayar Bayansan
Photos from: Pixabay.com

Serenity Prayer

God, grant me the serenity to accept the things I cannot change, the courage to change the things I can, and the wisdom to know the difference. Living one day at a time, enjoying one moment at a time; accepting hardship as a pathway to peace; taking, as Jesus did, this sinful world as it is, not as I would have it; trusting that you will make all things right if I surrender to your will; so that I may be reasonably happy in this life and supremely happy with you forever in the next.

Amen.

Reinhold Niebuhr

Dedication

Forty Days of Grace is the culmination of nearly 15 years of conversations with my best friend and heart-kin Wayne Hunter. Wayne died of cancer November 18, 2019. These daily readings are infiltrated, invigorated and oft times initiated by him.

Sitting by his bed, deep in the last conversation we ever had, talk went to this book. "Wayne you show up on nearly every page. I figured since you're too lazy to write a book, I'll just go ahead and use a lot of what you've come up with." With a sly Alabama grin he replied, "Why should I go to the trouble of writing, when I've got you to do all the work?"

It is indeed my honor to carry on the exploration of grace he and I started so many years ago. Our mutual quest changed us both, as we gave each other permission to wonder and wander into the land of possibilities.

On staff where we worked together we were often called by the other's name. Our discoveries became so intertwined it became easier to just say "we did" when asked who came up with a fresh notion. He showed up in my teaching. I showed up in his preaching. No ego. No competition. Just beautiful, brotherly collaboration.

So, Wayne, this book is for you. But more than that, even though you've not put actual pen to paper, it is also by you. You are my co-author; the voice in my head, the stirring in my heart, the footprints I find myself following, the presence in the room.

You should know that Wayne and I both began our exploration of grace as fear-driven shame-based followers of Jesus. For years we simply lived out the life we'd been raised in. Be afraid of God.

Be ashamed of yourself. Supposedly, these kept you both humble and obedient.

That is why this book explores both shame and fear. It assumes there are many others who are battling these same voices in their head: "God is going to get me. And I deserve it."

Everything changes once you fall into grace. It carries you into a fresh perspective of the scriptures. It transforms your prayer-life into a perpetual conversation with God. To think is to pray. It invites you away from judging and critiquing others and into exploring their beauty and uniqueness.

Grace is God's idea. His first move. He started this relationship (God-human). And if you follow the story in scripture, you see that he's always taken drastically gracious initiatives to draw us closer to himself.

The power and beauty of grace will gradually take on a definition unique to you as we move through these daily readings. Your openness to it will determine the degree of clarity and impact it establishes in you. God can express his love to you only as deeply as you allow him.

There came a time when Wayne and I realized rule-based religion was killing us. We couldn't do it right. It was then we began exploring the possibilities of grace. We invite you to do the same.

Introduction

For most of us, grace is a concept taught in religious circles. Something like: "God's unmerited favor." I suppose this is a good place to start, but it feels a little academic.

This book explores grace experientially, as if it is as real as gravity and the air we breathe. What if we lived in grace? What if it seeped into the cracks and crevices of our everyday adventures?

Many of us look through a blurred lens when we try to see God and how he feels toward us. We do the same with our self-image. Early on we were taught half-truths and un-truths about all this.

The result is usually fear and shame. We're afraid of God and ashamed of ourselves. Not much wiggle room wherein to experience grace here. The concept of grace is intriguing, but it likely only applies to bishops, saints and the pope himself. Everything inside us tells us we don't qualify.

This is why these readings begin with some pretty basic stuff, like shame and fear and wounds from our past. Until we discover where we are with these, we probably won't allow ourselves to live as if grace applies to us.

As we move along, you will be invited to do some writing (journaling). This will help you untangle the emotional bird's nest that tends to get wadded up in your mind, thus opening the way for grace to do what it wants to do. Honest clarity; that's what we're after.

These readings focus (though not entirely) on God and you. We start here because until you realize the passionate love God has for you, you'll not have authentic grace to share with others.

So, we start with you and God. Maybe a second book will be in order somewhere down the line that focuses more directly on how we live in grace with each other.

As dark as it may feel, our first reading deals with shame. It's where we start, because it's where most of us are.

One
Shame

Where are your emotions right now? Angry? Afraid? Depressed? Jealous? Discontented? Ashamed? Sad? Do you think any of these feelings are wrong? Are you weak for feeling them? Inferior? Stupid?

God gave you emotions. They are doing what he intended them to do ... telling you how your mind and heart are responding to your world.

Think of the people and events in your story. Some have trampled you under foot. People who should care, may not always be there for you. Promises that should be kept, are broken. Opportunities snatched away. Innocence stolen. At this point in your life, to feel nothing would be odd. It's entirely appropriate for you to feel anger, fear, depression, etc.

Shame is the one exception. You've messed up. We all have. Feeling guilty is the appropriate emotion for mess-ups. Shame goes too far. You feel guilty about what you did or didn't do. You feel shame for being you ... for existing. God gave you the ability to feel guilt. He didn't give you shame and he's never been good with it.

God made you. He put his spark of life in you. And when you arrived in this world, he said you were very good. Not one molecule of shame. You've hurt others and you've hurt yourself. Guilt? Sure. But not shame.

What you do does not define you. You are not your actions. At your core, you're still that person God created and called good. This is what grace says about you.

And this is where we begin our 40 days of grace.

If God didn't give you shame,
where did it come from?

Two

Back to Eden

According to the story, back in the beginning there was a garden called Eden where Adam and Eve, like two innocent kids, were naked and unashamed. God walked with them there.

God said it was all *very good*. But one day a lying snake showed up. This one could talk. Go figure? He told them if they ate fruit God had labeled dangerous, they could be better than the *very good* God had declared. They could be like God. They bought the lie and ate.

Wise old church people call this "the fall of mankind." Over the centuries many have used this story to make humans out to be a lot worse than we are. And have painted God as smaller than he really is.

Truth: God knew they'd eat the fruit before he ever created them. He created them anyway. God wasn't caught in a blindside. He was ready to forgive and heal. He's big that way.

Before he made you, God knew all the hurtful things you'd do and say. He created you anyway. He didn't do it so he could use you as a poster child for evil. Nor are you some vile mess he feels obligated to clean up. He created you, mistakes and all, so he could love you. Period.

His feelings toward you have never changed. The hurt you've given and received in your life has pained him. But he's never stopped loving you. You cannot make him un-love you. All he wants is to walk with you like in the garden. And he wants you to show up for those walks as you are, minus any fig leaves. (Adam and Eve's camouflage of choice)

Walks in a garden ... this is where grace brought humans and God together. It's where grace invites you.

Does your level of "bad" cause God
to think twice about walking with you?

Three

What about Jesus?

God is more mysterious than our brains can process. He is Father. He is Spirit. He is Son. Yet he's one God. Do the math all you want. It'll smoke your calculator.

So, what about Jesus? He is all human and all God; yet another brain bender. Conceived in a virgin's womb (no sex involved), he was born and grew as a human, like you and me ... until the day church leaders murdered him for being better than they could tolerate.

The God who used to show up in burning bushes and pillars of smoke and fire came and walked down our streets. He showed up at our picnics, slept in our beds and used our rest rooms. This gets our attention.

During a late-night conversation with a religious expert named Nich, Jesus unpacked the why of it all. He hadn't come to whip us into shape. He wasn't here to raise up an army against the evil Roman Empire. Far more personal.

Jesus said, *I didn't come to condemn. I came to save.* Jesus is for, not against you. He's not here to judge or pick you apart. He's your friend who has plans to hang out with you for the rest of eternity.

If you're battling shame and condemnation right now, it is not from God. It may be voices from your past. It may be the more toxic people in your life. But it is NOT God. Know this.

Our instinct screams that we need to do more good stuff to counterbalance shame. But you've tried that and your efforts run out of energy after a week or two. Maybe even sooner. How about let's not rush to sign up for some rigorous program of religious calisthenics. Jesus just wants you to trust what he said to Nich that night; that he came to love you to a better place. This is the power of grace.

Why might you personally struggle with self-condemnation?

Four

Fragmenting God

Yesterday we said God was bigger than we can grasp. But as we follow the story in the bible, it feels like he's getting smaller.

In order to be able to relate to us, he crawled into the box of time and space at creation. Up until then, he was limited by neither.

He focused himself on one small, insignificant group of people when he made a covenant with Abraham, father of the Jews.

Then there was Jesus who started out as a micro-fetus in a teenage girl's womb; traveled down the cramped birth canal and landed in a germ-infested cattle trough.

He forfeited the potentially "big" status of Messiah by hanging out with tax collectors and hookers.

And even as he told his disciples during their final meal that he knew of their betrayal, denial and scattering tendencies, he took on the role of a servant, got down on the floor, and washed their feet.

These days he offers his Spirit to live inside each one of us as our partner who does life with us.

Starting out as the mighty creator of the universe, God appears to chip off pieces of himself for our benefit with each new chapter in the story. But for some reason, as he appears to fragment, he feels more solid. While he's looking smaller, in reality, God is only getting bigger. The more he gives himself away for our sake, the greater he becomes.

Apparently, grace grows with generosity.

What kind of God do you need
when you're facing dark times?

Five

Forgiveness ... Clearing the Air

Jesus was teaching inside a crowded house. Some guys brought their paralyzed friend to him for healing. The doors were blocked, so they did what creative friends do, they ripped open a hole in the roof and lowered their helpless buddy down to Jesus.

Obviously, the man had a physical issue. Duh! But before the demolition dust had a chance to settle, Jesus told the guy he was forgiven. Almost like, "Let's get this guilt thing off the table so we can have clean air between us."

Peter, one of Jesus' disciples, asked how many times he should forgive someone who kept hurting him. Jesus shot back some crazy high number - like over 700. In other words, stop keeping count, just forgive.

When he was hanging on the cross, gasping for air, Jesus looked up and asked his Father to forgive those who mocked him as he died.

Forgiveness is God's thing. We're the ones who get twisted up over it. Our guilt creates awkwardness when we're around him. That's why he wants to get past that with forgiveness so we can start a more personal and relaxed conversation.

Forgiveness doesn't depend on whether we deserve it or not. It's about God wanting clear space between himself and us. If the big story in the bible reveals anything, it's that a desire for open conversation runs high on God's priority list.

If you have a history with rule-based religion you didn't get this version of God. Sorry! They needed their God to be harsh, or at least stern. What you heard about God has held you hostage since. Maybe it's time to rethink some of those old ideas.

Allowing God to forgive you will likely be your first taste of grace.

Do you struggle to forgive yourself?

Six

Feverish Emotions

We said back at the beginning that emotions are given to you by God. They tell you how life is impacting you. There is no such thing as a bad emotion. You feel what you feel. Period.

But ... like a twisted knee, emotions can become inflamed; swell up and get feverish. They no longer tell you how you're responding to life. They take over your life as the only voice in your head that demands your full attention.

You aren't just angry at your boss. You'd like to strangle him. You're not just depressed. You're thinking self-harm or even suicide. You're not just afraid. You're paranoid. Get the idea?

We've all been there; emotions with a temperature. They color outside the lines, step off the ledge, make really stupid decisions. The explosiveness of these emotions often shoves us back into our issues and addictions. We revert to our "drug of choice" in an attempt to calm down (shopping, working, eating, sleeping, isolation, substance abuse, self-harm etc.).

Where is God in all this? He understands. The story says, in the agony of facing crucifixion Jesus sweat like he was bleeding. He knows inflamed emotions.

Our instinct is to ask God to remove feelings that overpower us. Sorry, but that typically only fans the flames. Instead, tell God exactly how you're feeling and why you feel that way. If you want to hurt your boss, tell God why. Or try to convince him that suicide is a good option. Sounds ridiculous, but it works.

Spoiler alert! You'll be amazed at how simple honesty about your feelings will bust you wide open to grace. Grace is always there, but God will not barge in as long as you duck and hide. Give him some authenticity ... grace can work with that!

What emotions tend to go feverish in you?

Seven

Fear

What frightens you? Failure? Getting caught? Not knowing? Not being enough? Chaos? Pain? God? People? Crowds? Loneliness? Abuse? Ridicule? Yourself?

Here's a truth. Tattoo it on your brain. You are either driven by fear or you are driven by love. It is never both. It's one or the other. No exceptions.

Jesus' disciple John wrote that *love drives out fear.* He also referred to himself as *the one Jesus loved.* His heart was so full of Jesus' love, fear had to go. Fear is the strongest card the dark side can play in your life. God's love can overplay it every time. Your part in the game is to let him play it.

The dark side says, "You will fall back into your old ways."

God says, "Even if you slip, I will love you."

The dark side says, "You are a loser."

God says, "No matter how many times you fall, you're still my beloved and that makes you a winner."

If you let it, this truth will rock your world. At some point you're going to give in and let God love you. He won't force it. But he also won't stop trying. He's God. You're you. In the end, who do you think will win this lopsided standoff? You might as well let his love find a home in you.

Just to be clear, trying to love God more, is not what drives out fear. This approach only creates the new fear that you're not loving him adequately. Fear diminishes in direct proportion to you letting God love you. God loves you regardless of your behavior, your attitude or your mood. Live as if this is true and your fear will have to leave.

Of what are you most afraid?

Eight

Healing Grace

I'm hoping that by now you've moved past grace-is-only-about-forgiveness. Not trying to push. Just hoping. You may not have forgiven yourself, but at least in your head you understand that God holds nothing against you.

If grace is a meal, forgiveness is only the appetizer. The rest of the menu is a table spread out with "nutritional" grace, ready to heal you, to restore that which you've lost and mend that which was broken in you. Take it in.

You don't have issues or addictions because you're evil. You're in pain. Your favorite "medications" (control, work, shopping, rule-keeping, trying harder, substance abuse) take the edge off, giving short term relief. Problem is, each day you wake up and have to medicate all over again. Our human predicament.

Medication doesn't work because soul pain needs healing, not numbing. This is where grace comes in.

Where you are right now ... can you trust that God loves you even if you never change? This is a huge step in your healing. You don't have to change. You don't have to stop craving. You don't even have to stop "medicating." Just accept God's love for you. Literally.

Let this radical truth find a home in you. Saturate yourself with it. Give in to it. Let it seep into your thoughts and emotions. Living in the grip of this ridiculous love will make all your homemade attempts to medicate boring and tasteless.

Your surface issues are never your problem. Your inner pain is the real issue. Letting grace heal you at this depth will give you a new outlook. Start each day anticipating the healing work of grace instead of constantly begging for forgiveness. It will take time, but this approach will qualitatively transform your life.

What would it be like to wake up emotionally pain free?

Nine

Stepping into Healing Grace

Let's pick up where we left off. Our previous session was about letting God's love heal you. Now what?

Your emotions have been wounded. It started a long time ago. Like we've said before, wounded emotions refuse to behave themselves. They get all inflamed and demand a huge amount of attention. They will not be ignored.

At this point, you either keep numbing, avoiding or denying them or you take steps into healing. This begins by recalling some of your early wounds. God was there when they happened. God is here ready to heal them. Grace surrounds both then and now.

We mentioned in the introduction that writing helps in making sense of emotional pain and chaos. If you're inclined to write, here are some questions that might get you started.

-What happened back then?
-How did it make you feel at the time?
-What measures have you taken to protect yourself from that feeling since?
-How has it impacted the way you treat others?
-How has it shaped your opinion of God?
-How has it affected the way you view yourself?

This may be your first try at journaling. If you're going to explore grace, at least give writing a chance.

Healing grace doesn't have much to work with if you only share broad generalizations like: "I had a tough upbringing." or "I've had my share of bumps in the road."

Grace does its deepest healing when we write about specifics. Seeing details on paper can be painful, but this is essential in order for grace to do its best work.

How do you feel about revisiting some of the painful parts of your past?

Ten

God Loves You ... AND

We've been talking about healing grace. God is grace. So, God must also be our healer. But this is not a doctor (slash) patient arrangement.

God as doctor stirs up a whole new set of unhealthy thoughts and feelings. Like, he's never satisfied with your current state of health. And he won't be at all pleased until he gets all your vital signs exactly where he wants them. This feels like slipping back into chronic shame and fear. You're back to not-good-enough.

You are not God's project. You are his beloved. He loves you right where you are at this moment. And he will love you just as strongly even if you never change.

Legalistic religion tends to put a "but" in here somewhere. God loves you ... BUT you need to show signs of improvement. The truth is more like, God loves you ... AND.

God loves you AND he has complete and absolute confidence in his love. It is beautiful. It is relentless. It has held the universe together forever. It will find its way into your heart. It will never stop wooing you.

God is not just Father and Son. He's Spirit, which he promised would live inside you. Not a cell of your body is void of God's Spirit. He's not texting you love notes from somewhere above the clouds. He's in your veins.

But inside you he's not playing the role of an antibiotic that fights against something bad in you. It's more like he's a vitamin that builds up the life-force that is you. Even if you can't feel him, he's restoring you on the inside to your true self. The self you've always wanted to be. The self he's always known was there in you.

In your heart of hearts, who do you want to be?

Eleven

What about Sin?

You knew we'd get around to this one, didn't you? Yeah, if we're going to talk about God, we have to get around to sin at some point. But ... there are two different viewpoints on sin: legalistic religion's view and God's view.

Legalistic religion treats sin like a speeding ticket or drug bust. There are laws on the books. Break one and you pay. The punishment depends on the severity of the crime.

God doesn't give us rules to test us. He's not out to enforce his will with razor-wire fences or the long arm of the law. He's not some cosmic policeman who keeps a running rap sheet on us.

God simply wants to love us, like any good Dad loves his children. He's happiest when we embrace that love and then pass it on to each other.

But we're not always good at loving each other. We've been hurt. And hurt people tend to hurt people. When I hurt you, this hurts God. This is God's view of sin.

Sin is not breaking God's law. Sin is breaking God's heart. When I hurt someone, he loves (including myself) it hurts him.

Sin doesn't drag me into the courtroom to be judged. It takes me to the living room where Dad sits on the couch with his kids gathered around him. From time to time he has to give us that look, or pull us up beside him for a "talk." He loves us too much to just sit there while we hurt each other. Grace can do no other.

In spite of what legalistic religion has tried to teach us, our sins make God sad more than mad. He's sad, not because we're vile sinners. He's sad because we're hurting bad enough to hurt somebody else.

Why do you think hurt people hurt people?

Twelve

NOT a Commodity

Let's take a few days to talk about what grace is NOT. Grace is not a commodity.

Life as a human is one failure after another, even though we try hard to get it right every time. Never works! So, we find ourselves asking for God's forgiveness ... over, and over and over.

God has zero problem forgiving us. The problem lands in our lap. Nobody likes guilt. It usually festers into shame, which turns into a bad case of soul-flu. Who wants that? So, since God's forgiveness is the only cure, we tap that faucet.

It actually becomes a routine after a while. A pattern. Just walk over, turn the spigot and out it comes ... "You're forgiven." On our way we go, only to turn around and repeat the process.

After a while, it's like we form a subconscious sense of control over God's grace. Like we can turn it on and off as needed. Without realizing it, God's grace becomes a commodity. Really? We didn't set out to make this happen. We unwittingly settled into it.

Already you're backpedaling as you read. None of us would imagine we control God. Don't even want to try. And no, you don't need to crawl to God to beg his forgiveness for this messed up way of thinking.

Simply let God be God. He's trying to give himself to you all the time. You can't determine the *when*, the *where*, the *how*, or the *how much* of grace with the turn of a faucet. God's flow of grace is full and free and preposterously generous. It never stops or even slows down. What if you started focusing more on the full flow of grace instead of stressing over your behavioral indiscretions? Grace would gradually become your life (your world), instead of some commodity you turn on and off.

What if God is interested in your heart's intent more than your inability to get it right?

Thirteen

NOT a Business Deal

The justice system runs like a business. Break a law, pay the price. Commerce is the same; if you want a loaf of bread or a cold drink, you have to pay the price. This is the world where we live. Our culture. We know no other. Once a mind settles into this thinking, it naturally expects that God must operate the same. Do the crime, he makes you do the time.

Truth is, God would be in his rights to hold your sins over your head. But he doesn't. He doesn't because you're his beloved child. And though he does allow you to live with the outcomes of your sins, your poor choices never stop his flow of grace toward you. Tell yourself: "I'm God's child. He loves me in spite of my misbehavior. Better behavior will not make him love me anymore. Bad behavior will not make him love me any less. This is how good fathers love their kids."

Grace is not God's paycheck for good behavior. He doesn't withhold grace until he sees what he's looking for. He doesn't bribe you with it. He graces you full-on 24/7. You get all of God's grace all the time. In our world, this is considered bad business. But God is crazy that way. He is all about loving you even as you plot rebellion. He adores you no matter what you think, feel, do or say. You can't stop him.

David in the Old Testament, was a sexual predator who stole a man's wife, got her pregnant and then had the husband killed to cover his tracks. Horrid behavior! Yet, at the end of the day, God called him *a man after his own heart.*

In John's gospel, Jesus argued with Peter over Peter's upcoming denial. But Jesus' follow up: *Don't let this trouble your heart, I'm going to get a place ready for you, so we can be together forever.* If you're thinking about a fresh approach to your relationship with God, don't jump into frenzied behavioral improvement. Relax and let God love you even in the midst of your sin. Sounds lazy and irresponsible until you try doing it.

What about a God who will not un-love you?

Fourteen

NOT Lazy

Right about now, you may be asking what many have asked of both Wayne and myself ... "Isn't this grace thing a little too good to be true. Sounds lazy to me. So, I just sit down under a tree and watch God do all the work?" Apathetic! Presumptuous! Entitled!

Living in grace is about focus and attention. Each day, you have two choices. Do you concentrate on your performance? Or, do you focus on God's grace?

Mornings you wake up determined to be a better you than ever. The day unfolds. You're not doing so well. Temper. Lust. Fudging on the truth. But oh, are you ever trying, trying so hard your soul is sweating. By the time your head hits the pillow, you're a hot mess. Shattered expectations. Disappointment. Fear. Shame.

How's this working for you?

What if instead, you spent your days looking for God in every encounter, every person, every mistake and every success? In this way of thinking, he's "allowed" to show up however and wherever he wants. No religious or etiquette-driven restrictions. When your head hits the pillow after a day like this, you're not stressing over your performance. You're celebrating how creative and generous and beautiful God was all over the place all day long.

This is NOT lazy. This is intentional. This is going back to the original garden where we wait for God to show up and walk with us. Anticipation. Wonder. Hope. Exploration. Anything but apathetic or presumptuous.

Without coming off as sarcastic, can I challenge you? If you think living the grace-life is lazy, just try it for a few days. Then come back and tell me it's apathetic. Not focusing on your performance and looking for God instead is one of the greatest challenges you will ever face. But it is the way of grace.

For starters, try listing all the places
God showed up just yesterday.

Fifteen

NOT a Single "But"

You owe God nothing. He forgives you. He heals you. He encourages you. He sits and cries with you. He travels the valley with you. And he does it all with no expectation of payback. You don't earn grace. You don't pay it back.

If you were raised in legalistic religion, you're probably expecting a "but" right about now. By definition, if grace is going to be grace, it can't have any "buts."

Once grace leaves God's hands, it leaves his hands. His offer of love does not depend on your reception of it. You may mishandle it. You may ignore it. You may be transformed by it. None of these affect its flow. It just keeps coming. No "buts."

Grace is not one of several options God keeps in his back pocket. Like if grace doesn't work, he'll pull out the bullwhip and go to work on you, or maybe just walk away and let you self-destruct.

Grace is not about God trying to fix or reform us. Grace is God being God. He was this way before he created you and me. He'll be this way for eternity. You can test this. You can doubt it. You can ignore it. But you can't stop it. He just keeps being God.

God doesn't need you to need him. God doesn't need you to like or affirm him. He doesn't need to be recognized as the smartest or strongest or best person in the room. (We're so like this, it's hard to believe he's not.)

Foundational truth; when God gives himself to you, it's from a place of complete and solid confidence. He literally doesn't need anything in return. He just keeps giving himself away. This is who he is. This is what he does. No "buts."

How do you feel about a God who can grace you with no "buts"?

Sixteen

Jesus and His Posse

Jesus picked 12 guys to hang with for three years of ministry. They were everyday types. No licensed professionals. Like you and me, they weren't what you'd call house broken.

At the end of his earthly stay, just hours from his arrest and execution, Jesus gathered his crew together to share in one final meal. Sitting down to eat, he started calling them out. "One of you will betray me." "Peter, you'll deny me." "All of you will panic, scatter and hide."

But this wasn't Jesus raining down fire. Instead, he pulled out a towel and basin and got down on the floor to wash their feet. He also fed them bread and wine and told them this food and drink would serve as reminders of his life poured out for them ... so they could have hope and healing.

You and I are these guys. We've let him down. He knows exactly what we've done and will do. But instead of yelling at us, he wants to wash our feet and give himself to us so we can have hope and healing as well.

His guy Peter tried to stop the foot washing. Most of us resist this image of God's Son down on the floor. We've been far too bad, far too long. How about let's get a week or two of good behavior under our belts before we let him press in so close. This feels too extreme given the fragility of our shame.

Or what if we just gave up that old notion? We've held on to it for years and it has never served us well. What if we let Jesus go ahead and get started on our feet? At some point we're going to have to let God love us on his terms. It's either that, or we sit there in our dirt.

What do you tell Jesus when he reaches for one of your feet?

Seventeen

The Slow Work of Grace

Jesus was pretty impressive with his miracles. He walked on water. He changed it into wine. He fed thousands with a few biscuits and sardines. He healed blinded eyes and deaf ears, cast out demons. He even raised the dead. One guy had been gone so long he was beginning to smell.

The four gospels, Matthew, Mark, Luke and John, are full of these kinds of miracles. But for some reason Jesus didn't use miracles on his disciples.

They could have used some. One had raging trust issues. One was a thief. One battled impulsive fits of violence (chopped a guy's ear off). They argued over who was the boss; tried to gain advantage over each other. At one point they asked Jesus to nuke a group from a neighboring town they viewed as competition.

Like you and me, they had a way to go before they reached sainthood. And yet, Jesus never offered, or even proposed, a miraculous fix for their issues. Hmm?

John, in his gospel, emphasized that Jesus loved his disciples to the very end and promised he would never leave them. He had steadfast confidence that his love would have a deeper and longer lasting effect than any miraculous cure. The slow work of grace.

Have you begged God to take away your unhealthy habits, your crazy thinking, your bad attitudes, your tendency to make unhealthy choices? If he'd just grant you one miracle!

What if he sees you like he did his disciples? He's confident his love can deeply and profoundly transform you from the inside out. Trust the slow work of grace.

How are you with waiting ... on God?

Eighteen

The Power of Grace

Power is alluring. Some seek it through money, and then become enslaved by it. Others seek it through brute force, then go through life watching their back. In reality, every one of us is powerless, which makes us ideal candidates for the power of grace.

Grace can melt the heart of stone.
Grace can win over the skeptic.
Grace can forgive the worst crime.
Grace can heal the deepest wound.
Grace can comfort the lonely.
Grace can expose denial.
Grace can correct injustice.
Grace can reconcile broken relationships.
Grace can create beautiful art.
Grace can inspire courage and generosity.
Grace can bring order out of chaos.

Grace is God's heartbeat. God the Father, Son and Spirit harmonize with pure grace. It makes them one. It has for all eternity.

Grace created the universe, keeps molecules from flying apart, made you and me, gives us breath, greets us every morning. Even if you've never thought about it, you've been held by the power of grace your entire life.

You can resist it. You can criticize it. You can push back against it. You can question it. But you can't ignore it, at least in this moment. 'Cause right now it's got you cornered.

You can live without money. You can live without fame. You can live without much of what this world offers. But you wouldn't even exist in the first place if it weren't for the power of grace.

How would you explain the power of grace to a child?

Nineteen
Grace in You

Luke wrote a couple books in the bible. He wasn't a Jew like the other writers. Never met Jesus. Only heard about him. Being a doctor, he examined lots of people ... and he did it without ultrasound or CT scans. He relied on his trained senses and gut feelings.

As he grew to understand Jesus and grace, he couldn't help but notice shadows and whispers of grace in the patients he examined. At one point he wrote *the kingdom is in you*. He saw the grace that Jesus talked about even in those who were not card-carrying temple-goers.

Every human carries divine DNA. God gives his life to us. That's why he cheers at our conception, even if it is under less-than-perfect circumstances. God has always been in you and me, whether we're aware of it or not.

If the beauty of grace is already hiding in you, what would happen if you started looking for it? And when you spotted it, what would happen if you called it out, like maybe wrote something about it. Then, what would happen if you celebrated it, maybe in strong voice; with enough passion to make people think you're slightly touched? And what if you didn't care?

When you celebrate, it's not just for yourself and it's not just for God. The party is happening because you're finally realizing that the grace-life is about you and God linking arms and doing life together. Actively. Experientially. Moment by moment.

I can only hope that you're beginning to throw yourself into this adventure. But it's not like you have to go someplace far away to find it. Maybe for the first time in your life, you're discovering that grace has been messing around inside you all along.

*Think of a recent time you noticed grace
being active inside you.*

Twenty

Grace Partners

Grace is God giving himself to us. He gave himself to us when he walked with us in the garden of Eden. He gave himself to us in the law and the prophets of the Old Testament. And he gave himself to us in Jesus.

Toward the end, Jesus told his posse it was *better if he left them. Because if he did, he could send them his Spirit to be their partner.* (The word Jesus used literally meant partner - one who comes alongside.)

Partners don't rush ahead and expect you to catch up. They don't walk behind so they can watch and critique your progress. They walk beside you.

I'm messed up. I'm guessing you are too. Why would a God in his right mind sign up to be a partner with the likes of you and me? He knows our patterns. He's dealt with too many humans for way too long to be naïve about what he's getting himself in to. Yet he persists.

God doesn't have to swagger or strut. Jesus never did. But he is rock solid in who he is, what he can do and where he's going. He enters this partnership with complete confidence.

If this is true, your every day will never be the same. You can stop filling out proper request forms (shopping list prayers). You don't have to recheck the manual to make sure you're doing it right (fear-driven bible study). You're not dealing with a picky CEO. God is your partner. Just a thought away. Seeking mutual benefit. Eager to co-explore the possibilities of each moment.

This presents a life we've never even dreamed about: confidence without arrogance, joy in the midst of sad circumstances, hope in the face of bad news, generosity free from hidden agendas.

Just sit for a minute and let your mind take all this in.

What possibilities can you imagine
with God as your partner?

Twenty-One

Good Gifts

Jesus was the master of analogies, like his example of a parent tending to their child's basic needs. *If they ask for bread, you don't give them a rock. If they ask for an egg, you don't give them a scorpion.* Then he made his point ... *If you being evil know how to give good gifts to your kids, how much more will your Heavenly Father give his Spirit to those who ask.*

Somehow, we've come to believe that if God really loves us, he will give us good stuff. Cupboards will be full. Joints won't ache. Jobs will produce raises. Skies will be blue. Dreams will come true. In our minds, grace equals good fortune.

But this just isn't how life plays out. There must be something we're not getting here. What if, in the midst of the not-so-fortunate times, God gives us himself instead of "stuff?"

If what we said yesterday is true, you never face trouble solo. It's always with a partner who has already looked darkness in the eye and made it blink.

This means you never enter a strange room alone. You have a partner. You never face the results of a medical test alone. You have a partner. You never do life alone again. God walks beside you ... always.

God could easily buy us off with miracles, trinkets and treasures. Certainly, be less of a headache for him. And we'd still call it grace. Instead he gives himself to us, but not as a judge or boss or policeman. As messy as he knows it will get, he gives himself to us as our partner.

This is his idea. His initiative. We don't have to work to make any part of it happen. We simply take him at his word; act as if it is as true and reliable as death and taxes. (No, wait. That was a horrid analogy!)

During your darkest hour, would you prefer
God's presents or God's presence?

Twenty-Two

Healthy Ego

Alone, I'm all about me. And as long as I'm all about me, my ego runs the show. But at its best, my ego is fickle. It wants to be important, just not so important it has to do the heavy lifting. It wants to be liked, except not if it invades my privacy. It wants to appear strong without taking risks, to appear wise without doing the homework. Me. Me. Me.

In partnership with God, it's all about we. Facing life as a we, my ego finds its place. Success becomes a we thing. Failure turns into a we thing. I'm only responsible in my part of the we, not for the entire we. Life is a shared venture.

God, my partner, doesn't lay awake at night trying to figure out how to get people to like him. He was good on his own before I showed up with my insecurities. With him as my partner, I start sleeping better myself.

God is not crushed by criticism or ridicule. He's put up with that from the get-go. Facing these negatives with him as my partner feels more like a slight inconvenience. I don't have to take it personally.

A healthy ego, the notion is impossible. At least it was prior to grace. Imagine a day free from the need to be liked ... a day when slung mud rolls off like rain water. Painful conversations no longer hurt your feelings.

Do we even need to justify? What we're talking about here is gracious. Peaceful and blessed is a day lived with a healthy ego. It's like going back to the garden where I'm completely exposed, yet unashamed. Life is all about what's going on between God and me, instead of a constant obsession over whether I'm safe ... or right ... or liked. Grace!

What might a healthy ego look like for you?

Twenty-Three

Control or Cooperation

Let's go deeper with this idea of partnership with God's Spirit.

On your own, you have no choice but to take control of your life. If you don't make sure things turn out right, who will? You make decisions. You protect your future, your reputation and your stuff. Personal safety and comfort are up to you.

But because you're flawed, you miscalculate and mishandle. And the more jumbled it becomes, the more frantically you tighten your grip on control.

In partnership, life becomes about cooperation. Decisions are made together. The God of the universe steps in and shares your future, your reputation and your stuff. Safety and comfort are as much his concern as yours. And because he's God, he never mishandles or miscalculates.

Think of all the calories you've burned scrambling for control. It's robbed your joy, shackled you to your fears and shamed you when you failed. Trying to stay in control wears you down, and yet you persist. At some point, you look at your gauges and their running on fumes. You just want to give up.

Cooperation takes but one outreached hand. Joined with God who is never baffled or buffaloed, life becomes an adventure instead of a half-ton sack of rocks you drag out the door each day.

Each morning begins with you looking up from your cup of coffee at the Holy Spirit asking, "Where we going today?" To which he replies, "Wherever grace takes us."

How has trying to maintain control
worked for you so far?

Twenty-Four
Test or Adventure?

These daily reads ... can we just coast for a bit? This whole grace paradigm shift! Hopefully you're gaining momentum with possibilities you've never considered. The potential for growth stretches out ahead. Walking this grace-path can feel a little dicey. Here is yet another fork in the road.

Life is either a test you <u>have</u> to pass or it's an adventure you <u>get</u> to explore. You choose.

I hope I don't fall back into my old ways. (test)
Where will grace take me next week? (adventure)

I have to control my anger or I'll get fired. (test)
What does my anger tell me about me? (adventure)

I have to snap out of this funk or I'm through. (test)
Where is God in my depression? (adventure)

I must answer life's questions correctly. (test)
What am I learning these days? (adventure)

Do you see the difference? Life as a test is a constant struggle not to mess up. It goes nowhere. Just sits and stresses. Focus remains on you and your performance.

Life as an adventure means you jump into the flow of something bigger (grace). You're never certain what's just below the surface or around the next bend. Sure, you mess up, but that's no longer your focus. You're looking for the next discovery. And when you find it, you dive even deeper into it.

You may not dive perfectly, but you dive.

Why do we feel the need to grade
ourselves and others?

Twenty-Five

Grace is patient.

John wrote that *God is love*. By now we're figuring out that grace is love in motion. God isn't somewhere far away nursing sentimental feelings he has for you and me. He is actively expressing his love to each of us, all the time, close up. This is grace.

A late-comer to following Jesus was a recovering legalist named Paul. His life had been devoted to keeping and enforcing the law with deadly intent. One day grace caught up and knocked him down in the middle of a country road.

He was never the same. He wrote much of the New Testament, with several stellar passages including a treasure hidden away in a letter he wrote to the Corinthian church. Some call it "the love chapter" wherein Paul essentially describes grace.

Paul starts by saying *grace is patient*. Apparently, God doesn't get in a hurry. Nor does he panic. Begs the question, why am I so bent over instant perfection? Do I really have to get it right right now?

This isn't where most of us come from. We grow up feeling like God gives each of us 80 years or so. He plops a manual down and says get it right the first time or burn for eternity. And if you're born where there is no manual, you're pretty much toast from the get-go.

What parent expects this of a child? Healthy parenting does whatever it takes to help a child discover their potential, to introduce them to beauty, kindness, love, peace and joy, knowing each child will have to learn at their own pace.

God doesn't get in a hurry. Grace is patient.

How do you feel when God isn't fast enough to keep up with your expectations?

Twenty-Six

Grace is kind.

Some of us grew up thinking God was the exact opposite from kind, like maybe even a little on the mean side. At one point, I felt like a lab rat that he was testing. "How much can this guy take before he breaks?" Or maybe he was just trying to see what it would take to make me un-love him. This is part of my back-story. It may be yours.

Or, you may be one who thinks God has some explaining to do. Why doesn't he stop childhood cancer? Why does he let evil befall good people? A *kind* God would step up and do better.

If Paul is right ... if *grace is kind*, then how do we explain the pain of life? Where is God and his grace in that? Here is the context in which grace operates:

First, God willingly entered into our pain. He was born human. He grew up human. He was tortured human. He was murdered human. He's no stranger to human pain. He cries with us. He laughs with us. He doesn't wait outside our cave of misery for us to come out to meet him. He enters the darkness and sits down next to us. He didn't read about human suffering in a book. He lived it.

Second, God refuses to disrespect human freewill or the laws of nature. He doesn't normally overrule gravity, even when it involves an innocent person. And he won't overrule our freedom to choose, even when it's driven by dark intentions.

Grace doesn't prevent pain. Actually, it can't if God is going to respect our humanity and the world he created. Yet we've come to equate kindness with blue skies and pleasant paths. A kind and gracious God ought to make sure we are safe and happy. Always! In the end, know for sure that grace, though it doesn't eliminate life's valleys, always walks with us through them. Plus, it heals the wounds that may befall us along the way.

What would you like to say to God
about pain and suffering?

Twenty-Seven

Grace does not disrespect.

Grace never disrespects, discredits or dehumanizes.

Our world does. Factories grind up and spit out employees. Cultural disrespect aims itself at skin color, political divergence, socioeconomic standing, gender, sexual orientation, etc. In the name of Jesus, even legalistic churches dishonor those who don't march in lock-step with doctrine and etiquette. Dehumanization!

Grace seeks the best in others. Looks for the beauty. Celebrates the uniqueness. Explores the inner workings of God's Spirit in each person … every time, no exceptions.

But what about those awkward moments, when faced with a radically different person? Confusing mannerisms? Alternative values? Long pauses? Nervous silence? Opposing political views?

Typical knee-jerk reaction walks away, or jumps in to correct or fix. Both amount to veiled disrespect.

Turn this around toward God. Think of the silly awkwardness and nonsense we subject him to. And he just sits there waiting us out, with that Fatherly look on his face. As weird as we can get, he refuses to disrespect or dehumanize us.

Grace listens. It watches. It waits. It is present. It respects the person in front of you. As you patiently share in those clumsy, odd moments, grace grows powerful in you, cultivating confidence for your next non-typical encounter.

What would your part of the world look like if you decided to approach each people-encounter with the sole intention of helping the other person know they are loved and respected?

Just for fun, rehearse how you would "uplift" an awkward conversation.

Twenty-Eight

Grace is not easily angered.

There is a place for anger. If you're not angry at child abuse or rape or injustice toward the poor and needy, something is cross-wired in your thinking.

Chronic or hair-triggered anger, however, needs our attention. This kind of anger is fear-based, not love driven. When you become afraid you protect yourself by lashing out in anger.

Grace is not easily angered ... this statement is not telling us what to do. It's telling us how life can be. Where grace is, fear has to vacate. And once fear has left the building, there is nothing left to drive unhealthy anger.

This is not a rule against losing your temper. Neither is it a call to repress an emotion. Connect the dots. It's an invitation to allow God to grace you, full on, all the time. Grace in, fear gone. Fear gone; anger levels return to healthy.

(Anger can go two ways, outward against others and inward against yourself. Anger turned inward becomes shame. We already know, God is not the author of shame, nor is he good with it.)

You can expect natural outcomes to the grace-life. Your fuse will get a little longer each day. Explosions will become less frequent and produce less collateral damage. People will wonder what's up. Be ready to get real, 'cause conversations will ensue.

Imagine calm, objective conversations about anger. Anger as a topic instead of a raging emotion. Who knew? Swapping stories. Opening hearts. We're heading toward community, wherein healthy expressions of anger become the new normal.

How have you done at controlling your anger?

Twenty-Nine

Grace keeps no record of wrongs.

Memory ... a blessing and a curse. Back in the dusty files of your brain are snapshots, quotes and piles of documentation of every moment of your life. Some are accessible. Others are buried. They're all there.

Some of your memories are Gummy Worms. Some are Copperheads. The snake ones like to run the show. Panic. Rage. Shame. Jealousy. Depression. These serpents lurk under your bed. You never know where or how many. You just dread getting out of bed in the middle of the night.

The trick with poisonous snakes is to get them out in the open where you can see them. You can do this by journaling your *record of wrongs*. This forces them out in the open so you don't step on them.

Once you reach a comfortable stopping place with your writing, you might find someone with whom to share that part of your story. Invite them to listen, not fix or advise. This doesn't kill the snakes. It does defang them. Memories remain. Poison is gone. This is the hard-slow work that grace does inside you: pen to paper, sharing with a trusted friend. It's worth it. It leads to days spent not keeping score, not judging, not enforcing law and order.

If you're like most, this record keeping business has rented space in your head too long. Your radar is worn out from staying on high alert against additional threats. Stressful! The space between your ears has become so cluttered with infractions there's no room for grace.

Writing and sharing your *record of wrongs* opens you to healing grace. Remember, you don't work grace. You let it work in you. (Just for fun, every once in a while, try writing a "record of rights" about all the people who have loved and nurtured you over the years. Amazing results!)

Take some time to ponder your record of wrongs.

Thirty

Grace does not delight in evil.

Grace finds no pleasure in evil. Is not drawn to it. Is not entertained or intoxicated by it.

We generally link this word evil with cold-blooded killers, sexual predators or Satan himself, 'cause it provides a clear line of demarcation between them and "decent folks" like us.

Who would imagine decent people throwing a party over evil? No way. But what if Paul means something less dramatic when he uses the word *evil*?

What if evil equals any kind of un-grace: bigotry, stinginess, hatred, harshness, anything that dehumanizes another person, including the one in the mirror?

Remember, what we're talking about is descriptive, not prescriptive. This is not about what we should or shouldn't do. This is about what grace can be.

Grace forgives. Grace heals. Grace inspires. Grace transforms. A heart open to grace is a heart open to growth, change and discovery.

Fight against your own bigotry, stinginess and hatred all you want. You're not going to qualitatively change the way you feel. Only capitulation to grace can accomplish this.

While you sleep, while you're at work, while you're driving your car, grace is stirring around inside you. One morning you open your eyes and another unhealthy feeling has vanished. Your delight in gracious living is slowly and steadily overwhelming your delight in all things un-gracious.

Are there darker feelings you wish you didn't have?

Thirty-One

Grace rejoices in truth.

Yesterday we talked about unhealthy feelings you might have toward people. These dark feelings are almost always spawned by untruths. We buy lies told to us about others. Or we let single encounters define our long-term opinion of a person. These half-truths have been in our heads so long, they've calcified.

This doesn't make any of us bad or weird. This is what humans do. We cope with everyday life by clinging to preconceptions about the people we face every day. It's easier that way. Problem is, my preconception of you is not the same as the real you.

So, if I'm foggy about who the real you is, how can I grace you? (Or how can you grace me, if you're unclear about the real me?) It's impossible to love fake or altered versions of each other.

Grace doesn't know what to do with lies and half-truths in a relationship. There is nothing solid to work with, like trying to catch smoke in a net or get a firm foothold on an icy slope.

Always pursue truth. Truth about yourself. Truth about others. Truth about God. Refuse to believe something simply because it has taken up residence in your head or been told to you by a third party.

Ask personal questions of others. What's the real reason they did what they did? What is their back-story? Where do they hurt? What demons do they battle? Then there's self-examination. Why do I feel so strongly about a person or event? What does it remind me of from my past?

Ask honest questions of God. Allow him to be more than what others have told you about him. Invite yourself to imagine and ponder preposterous notions surrounding his love for you. (That's really what this book is all about, isn't it?) Then, whenever you know you've found truth, celebrate it with all your might.

*How do you personally decide
whether something is true or not?*

Thirty-Two

Grace always protects.

Protective grace ... always?

Does this mean grace creates a Nerf world? No sharp edges? Every fall is met with a soft landing? All pain and discomfort is thrown in jail as an evil villain. How's this work next to Jesus' promise that *in this world we will have trouble*? Let's explore.

We're all going to fall. Cuts and bruises are part of life. Grace enters the picture as it impacts how your heart handles the pain and inconvenience.

Grace doesn't diminish or demolish pain. It does use pain to remind you that you and God are partners, which means he's hurting right along with you.

In those dark moments, when your heart is bleeding out and God comes and sits next to you ... there's nothing like that. Those moments create fresh clarity about God's heart toward his children. Everything else in the chaos that surrounds you may be distressed, but grace has a grip on your heart.

Grace may not fix the issue, which is where our minds usually go with pain. Grace does fill our heart with all that partnering with God brings to the table.

But this isn't just about you. Grace applies to others as well. If you're actively exploring and experiencing grace, you will become increasingly aware of the people around you who are hurting. They're everywhere. Take the time to sit with them. Slow down and listen. Each of these encounters provide opportunity to explore and celebrate grace with each other.

Grace doesn't protect us against pain. It does provide strong support and confidence in our partnership with God and in community with each other.

How would you instruct a person to listen to the hurts of others?

Thirty-Three

Grace always trusts.

God has complete confidence (trust) in grace. It's not a roll of the dice for him; a maybe-this-will-work deal. He's not gonna pull out the big guns in case grace doesn't work. Grace has always been his plan "A". No need for a contingency plan. He trusts grace.

God also trusts that you will respond to grace. He designed you to need it. He trusts in the need he built into you.

So, you were made to need God's grace and God has infinite grace to share. Given the complexities of life, it takes a while for the two of these to find each other.

While God trusts grace, we start out trusting our supposed ability to be in control. We get good at it as children with demands, deceit, manipulation, stubbornness etc.

Over time we adjust to the unhealthy pattern of calling the shots, which is in reality our attempt to grace ourselves. Nobody knows better than I do what I like, what I need, what is essential for my happiness and wellbeing. We work this plan, often for decades, until we finally realize it's not working.

All along, grace has been trusting that you will eventually come to your senses ... that you will trust a God who has pursued you even when you acted like you didn't need him.

God never violates our freewill. Even so, he knows that our need for grace that hides deep inside will one day rise to the surface. We will have that moment of awakening and return home to the embrace of the Father.

Compared to God's grace, gravity is a shaky notion. To underestimate the weight and wonder of his love is not a trustworthy proposition. Trust the grace that already trusts in you.

What part of your life will fall apart
if you don't control it?

Thirty-Four

Grace always hopes.

Some people see hope as a wishing well. A luck thing. Odds are. Flip a coin. Heads or tails?

Hope turns to concrete when you mix it with grace. God is, without reserve, invested in you and me. Solid. I don't wish for it. I don't work for it. No need. It was going on long before I got here.

Hope is normally seen in the context of what is to come. "I wish this would happen." But combined with grace, hope essentially becomes a sneak peek into what's literally going to happen.

Somehow this feels like cheating. It's not really. The miracle of hope mixed with grace is not about knowing the events that will take place tomorrow. It is about knowing who will be waiting there for us when tomorrow gets here.

If you get nothing else from these readings, at least get this. Grace is God doing life with us. Jesus promised to never leave us. The Holy Spirit is our partner. Heaven is all about us being with God for the rest of eternity.

We're certain God has been with us every moment of our past. We're certain he is with us right now. And we have hope-based certainty that he will be with us tomorrow. He has a track record ... a credit score, if you will. It would be bad business on our part not to extend him a line of credit when it comes to hope.

If what we've been saying about grace up to this point is still just a concept to you, the solidity of hope will continue to elude you. Sounds intriguing, but you ain't feel'n it.

But, if you're getting caught up in the strong currents of God's love, this combination of grace and hope is turning into one of your rock-solid for-sure things.

What is your definition of hope?
What is your experience of hope?
Are they the same?

Thirty-Five
Grace always perseveres.

By now, at least in your head, you've processed that God's grace is in relentless pursuit of you. This is who he is. This is what he does. He's not about to stop.

Like we've been saying, what if this became your experience and not just an academic concept?

Life holds lots of pleasant things: sunsets, cotton candy, summer showers, polite conversation, cool shade, compliments, good hair days etc. But the expiration date on pleasant is short lived. Even the aftertaste has a fast-fade.

Grace sticks around. Stays with you. It doesn't run out of breath, sit down and tell you it will catch up with you later. Even when you're not feeling it, grace covertly invigorates and indwells you.

Grace is God in and with you. God has been around for an eternity. He's not going anywhere. He will be waiting by your bed when you wake up tomorrow. He is the air you breathe, the thoughts you think, the emotions you feel, the conversations you share. He is in your laughter. He is in your pain. He is in your clarity. He is in your confusion. We tend to fence God in. Relegate him to only the pleasant parts of life. This creates a fickle version of grace. Like grace is only present in the feel-good, but never the feel-bad.

Grace perseveres through it all. Hopefully, you are aware of it. Or, you can deny it. You might even ignore it. Doesn't matter ... it is still there, strong and pervasive, waiting to do what only it can do.

Positive emotions come and go like the wind. God is constant. Easy circumstances are mushy. God is predictable. There is our preferred happy version of grace. And there is God's version of grace. The resemblance between the two does intersect from time to time ... just not as often as we might think.

Are you typically aware that God is
close during your dark days?

Thirty-Six

Grace never fails.

We're at the close of Paul's "list." We already know God has confidence in grace. We know it's solid, relentless, powerful, etc. We end with *grace never fails.*

This entire book has been a series of forks in the road:

> *Do you want to be fear-driven or love-driven?
> *Do you want to live a "me" or a "we" life?
> *Is your life a test or an adventure?
> *Would you rather live in control or trust?
> *Are you going to try harder or fall into grace?

These all come down to one pinch point. Will you allow God to be who he says he is? Or will you keep negotiating; trying to create a more manageable version of him which allows you to maintain a semblance of control? Basically, keep on working night and day to prove you can handle things? In spite of all his legalistic education and duty-bound propensities, Paul eventually capitulated to grace. He was a smart guy. In the end, he figured out that grace was the only thing that would never let him down. Because, grace never fails.

> Keeping the rules – you fail.
> Striving for perfection – you fail.
> Fitting in – you fail.
> Fixing your issues – you fail.
> Sin management – you fail.
> Controlling others – you fail.
> Arriving at success – you fail.
> Managing your emotions – you fail.
> Loving others unconditionally – you fail.
> Perfection through knowledge – you fail.
> Brownie points for good deeds – you fail.
> White knuckling an addiction – you fail.
> Filling your heart's void – you fail.
> Creating your personal utopia – you fail. Grace never fails.

Where are you with grace right now?

Thirty-Seven

"Getting" Grace

So far, you've made your way through these 40 days of grace privately. You may have discussed your discoveries and questions with friends. But for the most part, you've likely flown solo. And that's okay.

Don't let reading this little book fool you into imagining that you suddenly get grace. We've only tiptoed around the edges. And ideas we've thought about have been articulated by a very flawed and limited human being. This isn't about any of us "getting" grace. This is about grace getting us.

God has had perfect grace with himself, Father, Son and Spirit for all eternity. No rebellion or squabbling. Nobody doing their own thing. Pure cooperation. When humans got here, God was able to show what grace looks like in the face of mutiny. He knew we'd defy him and was ready with grace.

How you handle that awkward coworker, your irate boss, your out-of-control child, the guy who stole your parking spot, all this is where grace has an ideal opportunity to get you and me ... if we let it. You will mess up. Grace has you. You will be confused. Grace will teach you. You will feel useless. Grace will verify you. Grace does life with you. Relax. Listen. Watch. When you recognize God's presence in a person or situation, call it out. When you recognize his presence in you, celebrate it.

This book has never intended to be "how to" in nature. There is no set method for grace. One does not formulate a grace-strategy. You simply allow yourself to get caught up in it. God initiates. You respond. When you do, grace starts showing up all over the place. In your mind. In your emotions. In your desires. In your relationships.

You don't pursue grace. Grace pursues you and when it catches you, you're caught up in something far greater than you ever imagined.

How has grace "gotten" you in these past few weeks?

Thirty-Eight

Everyone, All the Time

If what we're saying about grace is true in you and me, then it's also true in everyone. And it's true all the time.

Granted, people are open or resistant to grace on a variety of levels. And some people manifest the presence of grace differently than you or I do. But there is not a person on the planet who is not being graced by God full on, all the time.

In some religious circles we're told that we are the sole bearers of grace as we go out into a vile and sinful world. When we meet non-religious people, we alone bring grace to the encounter.

Once again, God has been shoved back into a box. We can't allow that God could be present or active inside a person if they can't produce the proper religious "credentials" or outward proof.

If God's grace is to be all that we've said it is, it has to be working inside everybody all the time. Otherwise, it's something less than grace.

Wow, this changes everything. I'm no longer just taking (or showing) grace to the person in front of me. I'm looking for it to be actively present in them. This means we instantly have something in common. Something to call out. Something to celebrate.

I'm not trying to persuade them, fix them, enlighten them or correct them. I'm entering into a dialog wherein we both share grace with each other. We enhance, empower and encourage each other eyeball to eyeball, instead of one being better or more "in" than the other.

This idea takes a while to settle in. We've been taught otherwise for too long. But given a chance, it completely transforms the way we love the person in front of us.

Think (in detail) about someone who is gracious, but not necessarily religious.

Thirty-Nine

Grace Story

You have a developing grace story. And whether you realize it or not, you want to tell it to a person you trust will hear it on the same level you share it. We need to know we matter to another human being.

If you have allowed yourself to honestly dig in with these daily readings, you've discovered more about yourself than you might have expected. At this point, you might want to seek out someone who wants to talk on this level of authenticity.

It takes grace to share your personal stuff. It takes grace to listen as well. Sharing often includes secrets. And telling secrets can feel like jumping off a cliff. Once you jump, you have no control over the outcome. You might land in a soft pool of acceptance. You might hit the hard pavement of rejection. You have to jump to find out.

Remember, the grace-life is an adventure, not a test.
If you're still doing the test thing, you'll likely keep quiet out of fear of rejection. But if adventure has crept into your veins, you're ready to explore new truth about yourself and grace.

Life is pretty rough. We've built solid walls around our secrets. Your wall might be rudeness, humor, wordiness, silence, lies, complexity, a stone face. We each create our own way to keep people out.

But ... here you are, ready to dismantle some walls. The first brick is always the hardest. Once demolition gets started, the sledgehammer finds its natural rhythm.

Grace will likely never be more than an interesting idea if you ponder it on your own. Step out of isolation. Share. Trust. This may frighten you to death, but it will help grace close that strategic gap between your conceptual head to your experiential heart.

What is the first brick you will remove from your wall of protection?

Forty

Be Real - Be Loved

Here we are at the end of our conversation. It's been a pleasure traveling with you. I may not know you, but I appreciate and respect you. We may meet some day. I hope so. At the close of these readings, how about we boil this down into two simple statements:

Be real.   Be loved.

You've invested forty days into getting real with your thoughts and feelings about God, your past, your issues, your relationships and your pain. If you've faked your way through this, bless your heart. You missed out. But if you've told the truth, a dam is already crumbling inside you. Grace and truth are flowing ... gaining momentum My deepest hope is that you now know God loves you. The grace-life is not about you getting it right, upping your game or trying harder. It's not even about you loving God and others better than you used to. It's just about letting God love you.

Be real. Be loved. So different from the life most of us live, which is more like:

Be better. Be tolerated.
Be strong. Be feared.
Be smart. Be respected.
Be good. Be rewarded.

At some point you realize this old way doesn't work. Never will, 'cause it's impossible. You can't do it.

As you walk into authenticity, you realize this is something you can actually do. The huge bonus comes when you also realize God and other people genuinely love and adore the real you. Like others who have opened to grace, you may be wondering what's next. Just step outside and get started. Grace only gets stronger the longer you live it.

How will you live in grace today?

Made in the USA
Columbia, SC
21 February 2020